EXPERIENCE

MISSION TRIP DEVOTIONS & JOURNAL

Standard®
PUBLISHING
Bringing The Word to Life

Published by Standard Publishing, Cincinnati, Ohio
www.standardpub.com

Project editor: Kelly Carr
Cover and interior design: The DesignWorks Group
Printed in: China

ISBN 978-0-7847-2190-2

13 12 11 10 09 08 07   9 8 7 6 5 4 3 2 1

SOMETHING UNEXPECTED

What have you gotten yourself into? You've just begun to experience your mission trip, and you never know what could be in store for you.

Sure, you've made plans. You've got work projects scheduled or outreach events designed. But you know how life is—there's always something unexpected, no matter how much you plan.

God works like that, doesn't he? He has a way of getting our attention and reminding us to stop relying on our own talents, brains, or muscles and start relying on him.

So go ahead and plan now to fully experience whatever God has in mind for your trip.

Whether you're nailing together two-by-fours in the Midwest or doing a puppet show for Muslim children in the Middle East, every situation is an opportunity for you to learn from God and be used by him for the greater good of his kingdom—if you are willing.

EXPERIENCE

And that's the mystery you are about to experience—God showing up in ways you never would have imagined, using you to do things you never could do on your own.

That's the fun of serving God. You can never fully plan, prepare, or anticipate his power. But you can revel in the blessing of being a part of his work here on earth.

This book has fifteen devotions and journaling space to help you dwell on the things you experience during your mission trip. As you see, hear, and feel God moving, record your thoughts; read and be challenged by God's Scriptures; ponder the growth happening in, around, and through you.

These devotions were written by people who have served the Lord both in the U.S. and in places beyond. They share what God has taught them in order to help you listen to the Holy Spirit speaking to you during your journey.

Experience what God has in store for you.

SCAFFOLDS

by Jason Casey

Have you ever watched painters set up
for a job on the outside of a building? I don't
mean just noticed—but really watched. And
I don't mean the kind of painters who use
a ladder to work on a two-story house but,
rather, the kind of big crew that completely
surrounds a building with scaffolding. Have
you ever watched them?

Scaffolds—they are all over Italy. Drive
around any city here, big or small, and
you are certain to see buildings in various
stages of being remodeled. In this country,
remodeling requires scaffolds. You see,
most people here do not live in independent

houses but in apartments inside of several-story buildings. Instead of each homeowner running to the local hardware store, choosing a color, and painting, each apartment owner votes. Together all the tenants decide on one color and style for the entire building. That's when the work begins.

UNVEILED GLORY

Before I left to go to the mission field, I heard a statement made during a training session. The person said that the reason we were going to the mission field was to be conformed to the likeness of Christ (Romans 8:29). I doubted that conclusion and thought to myself, *I'm going to the mission field to start a church!* I'm sure others thought, *Well, I'm going to the mission field to win people to Christ!*

But it turns out that nothing could have been more accurate than that likeness-of-Christ statement. We are all in the process of being refined, conformed, and renovated. Whether we're on a short-term mission trip, actually living in a foreign country, or going through the daily grind at home, that process is still happening.

I love what Paul writes in 2 Corinthians 3:18: "And we, who with unveiled faces all reflect the Lord's glory, are being transformed into his likeness with ever-increasing glory, which comes from the Lord, who is the Spirit." Here Paul is referring to the time when Moses was with God on top of Mount Sinai (Exodus 34:29-35). When Moses came down the mountain, his face was radiant from having been with God—so radiant, in fact, that the people were afraid to come near, and Moses was forced to put a veil over his face.

Can you imagine having an encounter like that with God? Back to 2 Corinthians—Paul

says that we who have *unveiled* faces (*we* don't
have to hide away God's brilliance that's on
us!) all reflect the Lord's glory and are being
transformed. We're being changed like a
caterpillar that undergoes a metamorphosis
when it enters the cocoon looking and behaving
one way and exits a different creature.

TRANSFORMATION PROCESS

Here in Italy, when painters arrive at a
building that needs to be renovated, they
first set up all of the supplies they need.
They stack hundreds of poles, planks, and
braces. They bring in crates of brackets and
loads of tools. All of this is just to put up the
scaffolding. The process takes days, if not
weeks. They start at the bottom and slowly
wind around the building, level by level,
creating ladders and walkways to connect the
whole network, until the entire building is
covered up. The final touch is to wrap all the

scaffolding in netting or fabric. At that point, you can no longer see what the old building looked like.

Next, they scrape off all the paint that is chipping. Then they come in with a heavy-duty gas torch and heat up any old paint that is still on the wall, until it becomes so hot that it can be taken off like butter with a scraper. At the end of the day, there are huge piles of old, curled up paint pieces at the base of the building and all over the scaffolding, and the walls are back to smooth concrete like on the day the structure was first built.

Then experts come in and check the walls for stability. Everywhere they find a weak spot they mark it, and other workers have to come in to tear out and rebuild those sections of the walls. A power-sprayer is then used to clean off any excess paint and to bring the marble and brick sections of the building back to pristine condition. In the end, layers of paint and texture are applied before all the scaffolding is taken down.

And when the scaffolding comes down, what a glorious sight! The whole street is affected; people walking or driving by stop to notice. Neighbors will talk about the building that has been renovated. What was once an eyesore now is new and reflects the glory of the Mediterranean sun.

SPIRITUAL RENOVATION

Through your mission trip, you are willingly putting yourself in a new situation and environment where God can mold you and change you. The beauty of following God is that he has already chosen what he wants you to look like when the scaffolds come down. He knows where your walls are weak. He knows what color and style best suit you! But the process is not easy. It's even painful at times. Old ways and whole parts of you will need to be heated and scraped off. The crustiness of the way you used to be will need to be washed off.

Slowly you will begin to appear as he wants you to appear—which is like *him*! As the scaffolding comes down, you will reflect the glory of God just as Moses did, and all those around you will notice. This is absolutely essential if you are going to be involved in sharing God's grace with others. The message you have to share, of how God longs to renovate everyone, starts with you and with how that message is being lived out in your life.

Are you willing? Will you let the process begin? In this renovation, one of your most valuable tools is the willingness to be changed. You can, after all, always reject the scaffolding and the repairs. You need to be vulnerable, letting the world catch glimpses of what you look like under the surface. You have to believe in the designer and his plans. And finally, you will have to do some of the work yourself! You will need to spend time reading God's Word, which has countless examples of how he has continually been in the process of changing people. Take notes along the way. Share with those around you how God is changing you! And trust that when the scaffolds come down, you will reflect his glory.

Praise God for his beautiful design and excellent work in your life. Ask him to continue working and to give you patience, wisdom, and strength. Finally, ask God for his Spirit's guidance as you have opportunities on your mission trip to share with others what he has done in your life.

My Experience

_____
_____
_____
_____
_____
_____
_____
_____
_____
_____
_____
_____
_____
_____
_____
_____
_____

My Experience

DEMOLITION

by Ben Hedger

The demolition process is one of the most exciting jobs to experience. Tearing down drywall, smashing concrete, and ripping shingles off a roof are all part of removing the old in order to replace it with new material. Many people seem to enjoy this process for a couple of reasons.

First, little precision is needed to destroy the selected object before them. The second reason deals with satisfaction. There is a sense of accomplishment when a room is prepared for new drywall, when the cracked sidewalk is removed for smooth concrete to replace it, or when new shingles can be applied to a roof.

Demolition is important because it starts a necessary process. Tearing down the old has to happen so the inside structure can be examined. We remove items and materials that are worn out. And only then can we start fresh and apply a new façade.

DESTROYING SATAN'S STRONGHOLDS

In Scripture Paul wrote about a demolition process. But he was writing about more than tearing down physical walls, breaking concrete, or ripping off shingles. Read 2 Corinthians 10:3-6.

It is clear that Paul was not renovating his home or repairing his roof. His idea of demolition involves the spiritual battle that Christians encounter each day; he talks about destroying the walls that Satan and our own sinfulness create between us and God. The demolition Paul writes about doesn't require a sledgehammer or crowbar but, rather, weapons that "have divine power to demolish strongholds" (v. 4).

Do you want to battle Satan and sin using minor tools—or the weapons that God makes available? Ephesians 6:10-18 discusses the tools that Christians have at their disposal. Weapons of prayer, faith, hope, love, God's Word, and the Holy Spirit enable each person to tear down spiritual barriers.

Think of a time when you fully equipped yourself with God's tools to enter spiritual demolition. What tools did you use to work through your destruction of struggle and temptation? When you look back to your experience, what did God teach you through the battle?

EQUIPPING YOURSELF

Whether you are part of a construction project in Memphis or leading a VBS in

Brazil, remember to equip yourself with the proper tools for the immediate task. Repairing a home and teaching a lesson require different tools but the same focus in order to share God's love.

What current strongholds do you need to demolish? How is Satan trying to keep you from sharing the love of Christ? As you serve the Lord on your mission trip, use the demolition weapons God provides to enter the battle with confidence.

Pray today that God will equip you to demolish whatever is keeping you from completing the task he has called you to do.

My Experience

My Experience

ACTIONS OF FAITH

by Kelly Robison

Hebrews 11 is a chapter of the Bible filled with names of people who acted upon their faith in God. The people were not perfect by any means. They sinned. But they are noted for putting their faith into action. One person on that list is a prostitute named Rahab (v. 31).

Rahab became a character in a story that actually began before she was born. God had used Moses to rescue his people, the Israelites, from slavery in Egypt. God promised that they would live in a much greater land than Egypt; however, this did not happen right away. The Israelites had to wander in the desert for forty years as punishment for their rebellion.

The book of Joshua begins just as the Israelites' time of wandering was coming to an end. God appointed Joshua as the leader of the Israelites, and he told him to start scouting out the promised land that they would receive, including a city called Jericho. This walled city was the home of Rahab.

IMPERFECT PEOPLE

In Joshua 2:1, we are introduced to Rahab and her ungodly profession. Why do you think God used a prostitute to help carry out his plan for the Israelites? I think this illustrates something very significant about God. He uses whoever is willing to be used! He uses anyone who will obey him in order to reach those who need him. Rahab was a woman with a past, but she ended up being faithful to a God she didn't know.

God wants all people to be obedient and filled with faith in him, no matter what sins and scars their pasts may hold. Just like Rahab, there are things in my past I wish I could erase—words I've said to hurt other people and things I've done that I knew were wrong. You can probably think of sins in your own life that you aren't proud of.

Rest in the knowledge that even though you've made mistakes, if you are a follower of Jesus, you have been cleansed by his blood and can be forgiven. God wants to use you in spite of the messiness of your past!

God doesn't look for *perfect* people to use; he looks for *willing* people, and he will use anyone who makes himself or herself available. Everyone with you on this mission trip is imperfect, but your willingness to be used for God's glory is the key.

DANGEROUS REQUEST

Take a moment to read Joshua 2:2-11. Rahab hid the Israelite spies in her home, even though she knew that if she were caught, she could be killed for her actions. She might have been scared, yet Rahab still took the chance that the God of the Israelites might be someone worth serving. Although she may not have even realized the magnitude of her actions, God used Rahab to help his people.

Rahab was honest with the Israelite spies! She could have pretended it was no big deal for her to hide them on her roof, but she didn't. She told them that their whole city was afraid of them and the power of their God.

Sometimes God asks us to do things that make us scared or uncomfortable. These things are good for us (even if we don't like them at the time!) because we learn a lot from them. We learn how to trust God more, and we learn to obey even when it's hard. I remember being both excited and scared when I went on my first mission trip. When I returned home, I knew I had changed—and I was so thankful I had gone, in spite of being nervous.

Were you nervous to sign up for your mission trip? Sometimes being willing to be used by God means doing something new, something out of your comfort zone, or maybe even something dangerous. But your experiences will help you to grow in your faith because you will be putting your faith into action.

GOD'S TIMING

Read Joshua 2:12-24. Rahab knew that Jericho was going to be destroyed, so before the spies left, she asked for a way that she and her family might be saved. The Israelites promised that if she told no one about their visit and followed their instructions, she and her family would be saved.

Every time I read this account, I am struck by the fact that she didn't just ask to go with them then! If I had been Rahab, I think I might have left the city right away. She lived in a home built high into the city walls of Jericho. She knew that, shortly, this city would be destroyed and the walls would come crumbling down around her. But she stayed, and she trusted this foreign God and his people to save her and her family.

Now read Joshua 6:17-25. The entire city of Jericho was destroyed by the Israelites, but Rahab and her family were saved. Rahab didn't know exactly how it was going to work, but she hoped that God would save her because he had promised through the spies.

God is faithful, and he asks that we be faithful as well. He wants us to obey when he asks, not just when it's convenient or easy. Maybe you had to make some sacrifices to come on this mission trip. God sees your actions and knows your heart. When you are faithful to him, you will be blessed.

IMPORTANT OBEDIENCE

Rahab's willingness to take a chance on God and act on faith changed her forever. In fact, her story of faith did not end when her life did. Take a moment to read Matthew 1:5, 6.

It's easy to skip over genealogies. Sometimes they seem like pointless lists of names, but they're not! These names tell an important story of faithfulness that leads to something greater. Matthew 1 traces the ancestry of Jesus. Did you know that Rahab was Jesus' grandmother, with more than twenty-five *greats* in front of it?!

Her faithfulness allowed her to be in the family tree of the coming Savior, Jesus Christ.

Sometimes we wonder if our actions are important. Rahab was probably glad that her faithful actions led to her family's being saved the day Jericho was destroyed. But she had no idea that her faith would be part of the process that caused the entire world to be saved through Jesus!

The time you spend serving on your mission trip may not feel like a big deal when so much in the world needs to be changed. But your faithful actions are significant! The effects of your service will reach beyond what you will ever know. You have been obedient to God's call, and you can't imagine what he will do as a result.

Take some time to praise God for who he is. Thank him for the generations of faithful followers from way back in biblical times whose actions have eventually led to your hearing about Jesus. Thank God for loving and using all of us, despite our sins. Ask him what actions he needs from you on your mission trip. Then commit to doing those actions in faith.

My Experience

ALL FOR THE GLORY

by Lindsey Bell

When I was in high school, I often struggled with my purpose. *Why am I here? What is God's will for me? What am I supposed to do for the rest of my life?* Questions like these haunted me, and it didn't help that many of my friends already seemed to know what they were going to do with their lives. For years, I felt lost when I thought about the future.

But then I read Isaiah 43:7. In this chapter God talks about how he is going to rescue his people. He says he will protect "everyone who is called by my name, whom I created for my glory, whom I formed and made."

And it hit me—we were all created for God's glory. That is our ultimate purpose. How we specifically do this (such as which job we take, where we go to college, or whom we marry) will flow naturally from seeking to glorify him daily. When we seek to bring him glory, he will guide our ways so that whichever road we choose, we will ultimately end up right where he wants us.

Have you ever struggled with knowing your purpose? Do you still? Can you think of a time when you knew you were fulfilling God's purpose for your life? How did this make you feel? Was your decision to serve on this mission trip made for God's glory?

JESUS' EXAMPLE

In 1 Corinthians 10:31, Paul challenged the church in Corinth with these words: "So whether you eat or drink or whatever you do, do it all for the glory of God." Notice that it doesn't say "only when you sing praises" or "just when you read your Bible." Instead, it says, "*Whatever* you do, do it all for the glory of God."

Those words apply to your mission trip: When you take a bite of that mystery meat your foreign guests are serving you, eat it for God's glory. When you share your testimony with that person on the street, tell it for God's glory. And when you suddenly realize you took time out of your summer to do tasks that others might think are meaningless (like mixing bag after bag of concrete), do it for his glory.

Jesus recognized that even his purpose was to bring God glory: "I am not seeking glory for myself; but there is one who seeks it, and he is the judge" (John 8:50).

Think about it—Jesus, who was with the Father in the beginning; Jesus, who is the

King of kings and Lord of lords; Jesus, who is the beginning and the end, did not seek glory for himself. If anyone had the right to do so, it was he who was God in the flesh. But he didn't. The Son of God showed us how to live in a way that would give glory to the Father.

MY PRIDE

If Jesus didn't seek glory for himself, then we definitely shouldn't. But it's not always easy. I remember a time when I didn't give glory to God.

I did not grow up going to church. My family started attending when I was about ten years old, and we quickly realized how little we knew about the Bible. As a result, my family and I dug into the Scriptures. We soaked in as much of the Bible as we could contain, and in doing so, I memorized a lot of Scripture. Though it's embarrassing to admit, as my knowledge expanded, so did my pride.

One time, my Sunday school class divided into teams and played a game to see which team knew the most Scripture. We went around the room, and each team had to quote a Scripture. If a team couldn't think of one, they were eliminated from the game. My team ended up winning the game, and as you may have guessed, my pride swelled.

I had yet to learn what John the Baptist had discovered: "He must become greater; I must become less" (John 3:30). Thankfully, the Lord has since shown me that knowledge is a gift from him. I can know nothing unless he enables me to learn it. And my knowledge is not because of my own greatness but because of God's goodness to me.

Consider this—God doesn't give us gifts so *we* can receive glory. He gives us gifts so we can use them to give *him* glory. You're not a talented athlete only because you practice hard. You're not an enthusiastic speaker because of your own natural speaking ability. You're not a talented musician because of your own greatness. Any talent you have has been given to you from the Father, and he gave it to you to use for his glory.

Can you think of a time when you have taken the glory for something God did in you or through you? Why do you think it can be difficult to give glory to the Father for good things we do?

THE FATHER'S REFLECTION

About a year ago, I was standing in the meat department of a grocery store, when a man approached me and asked, "Are you a Christian?" His question caught me completely off guard.

I had seen the man earlier and helped him pick out a bottle of shampoo. (He said his wife had recently passed away, and she normally did the shopping). Reading a few shampoo labels wasn't anything special to me, but the man explained that he could tell I was a Christian because I had taken time to help him. It only took a minute, yet my small, seemingly insignificant action had reflected the Father.

The Lord must have kept me from rushing by the man, because I am typically in a hurry. I was privileged to bring glory to the Father that day, and I may never know how much of an impact my actions had on that stranger.

But isn't that how God often works? We do something small, and he works to make a huge impact. My question to you (and to myself) is this: When you achieve something great, will you refuse to take the glory and instead give it all to the Father? Someone's eternal state may depend on our answers to this question.

YOUR CALLING

Think of the gifts and talents God has given you to use for his glory—not just the obvious ones but perhaps any off-the-wall abilities God has given you as well. For example, maybe you can ride a unicycle. Or you might have the ability to whip up a pot of homemade vegetable soup in exactly twenty-two minutes! And what about your beatboxing skills? God can use any of these for his glory!

Have you been using your talents for the right reasons? What are some practical ways you can give glory to God on this mission trip?

Take some time right now to meditate on God's glory. Next, praise God for the knowledge that his ultimate will for you is to bring glory to his name. Pray for God to remind you of this and to give you peace during times when you question your purpose.

Recognize that your actions (both on this mission trip and every day) are significant and that God can cause anything you do to have an eternal impact. Ask God to remind you that he is the one who deserves all the credit for anything good you are able to do.

Finally, praise God for the example of Jesus, who sought the Father's glory rather than his own. Commit to following his example by doing everything in such a way that it brings glory to the Father.

My Experience

UP ON THE ROOF

by Bill Baumgardner

Over and over again, it's my privilege as a leader of service projects to share with others the reason that students are seeking to help them: they love Jesus Christ! I tell people that the students want to follow in his steps by serving others. In doing this, Jesus' name is glorified.

And that's one of the great things that happens when you serve others—Christ is lifted up. In John 12:32, Jesus said: "And when I am lifted up from the earth, I will draw everyone to myself" (*NLT*). He was indicating that he would be "lifted up from the earth" to die on a cross (v. 33). But there is something about that concept of Jesus being lifted up. When our actions lift up the name of Jesus, he will still use that to draw people to himself.

A NEW VIEW OF CHRISTIANS

During a Christmas break several years ago, I led a group of students to Florida to help the victims of several hurricanes. It was overwhelming to see all the damage that had been caused by the winds. When we flew in to Orlando, all we saw were blue tarps on the roofs of homes.

We helped one family of six that had sustained severe damage from three hurricanes! The first hurricane took the roof off their home, and the other two hurricanes dumped tons of water into their house. All the drywall and insulation was soaked, falling, and moldy. To make matters worse, the family's insurance company went bankrupt and left the state. The family had no money to repair the house.

The family's neighbor had called to ask whether our students could help out. When we said yes, the neighbor then had to convince this family that a bunch of Christian students and sponsors would help them. After some resistance, they agreed to let us.

The students worked hard for three days. They tore off what was left of the roof and replaced it entirely. Walls within the house were gutted and replaced. By the time we had to leave, the roof was completely done, and a lot of the interior walls were fully restored.

As I stood on the roof with the homeowner, he was amazed at what had happened in those three days. He said, "I almost didn't let you guys help me out. To me, Christians are hypocrites. They say one thing but do something else. But these people practiced what they preach. I have a new view on what Christians, especially Christian young people, are all about. Thank you!"

As we departed, I prayed that the man and his family would continue to encounter real Christians whose actions live out the faith that they claim.

DISCOVERING TALENT WITHIN

Another great benefit in ministering to others is that you find out more about yourself. You discover what gifts and talents God has given to you.

During another mission trip in New York, we were in charge providing a chapel service for a mission to the homeless. I asked a young man in our group to give the devotions that evening. He was scared; he had never spoken in front of anyone before. After receiving lots of encouragement and prayer, he decided to do it, and he did a great job! A few years later, I saw that same young man at a Bible college, standing in front of a crowd and using the speaking talent that God had given him. From serving in that mission, he learned about a gift with which God had blessed him.

What new things have you discovered about yourself so far on your mission trip? What talents has God blessed you with that you didn't realize until now that you had?

KEEP YOUR EYES OPEN!

Lifting up Jesus and discovering a new talent are just two of the many benefits in serving God. Keep your eyes open on your trip, and you'll have the opportunity to learn other benefits of serving our great God!

Praise God for allowing you to grow and learn and honor him through serving others on your mission trip. Thank him for the talents and abilities he has given you that you can use for his glory.

Pray that God will help you to continue living out your faith in such a way that people who don't follow Jesus can learn that Christians are sincere. Commit to God that you will always lift up the name of Jesus—then do it!

My Experience

My Experience

DREAM BUILDERS

by Katie Runner

Have you ever worked on a team that included a few people who were difficult to get along with? (Maybe you're dealing with that right now!) Have *you* ever been one of the difficult ones on a team? (Be honest!)

I remember a time when I was a terrible teammate. The disagreement I had with my fellow team member was over something silly that I don't even remember now. However, I do clearly recall my selfish response and my harsh words in our conversation. After our argument, I retreated to my room where I started thinking, *I can't believe she acted like that!*

As I sat in my room, stubbornly thinking of all the reasons she had done me wrong, conviction slowly crept over me. I realized, *I was just the biggest jerk.* I knew that I needed to go back to her. It felt like it took every muscle in my body to step from the room and return to my friend. But as I apologized for what I did, the results were amazing. A genuine closeness came between us that was greater than anything we had before. When we invited our unbelieving Turkish friend over later that night, the evening was full of laughter and joy. Mission accomplished!

COMMON LOVE

Healthy teams are vital to effective ministry. God has created us to work together, love each other, and bring others to him through our unity. Jesus said to his disciples, "A new command I give you: Love one another. As I have loved you, so you must love one another. By this all men will know that you are my disciples, if you love one another" (John 13:34, 35).

That verse came to mind last year when my friend Amy was leaving to be a missionary overseas for two years. A little girl at church said, "Amy, I'm gonna pray for your team that they will love each other so that people will know Jesus." This young girl knew something that it has taken years for me to figure out, and I still do not fully understand—somehow, through our love for each other, people see the love of Christ. God uses our love for fellow believers to demonstrate his own love for all people.

One of the reasons another friend of mine, previously a Muslim, became a Christian is because of the love she saw between a husband and wife and their love for their children. She said, "I've never seen such love anywhere. I knew there was something here that was different." As believers, loving others is a strong testimony to the love of God. As we love the people we are closest to, it points others directly to God.

COMMON MISSION

God's heart is for all nations. As you work together with a team on your mission trip, remember that you are serving God, and remember the great love God has lavished on you. He did not give that love just so you could feel good about yourself. He loved you so that you can know how to love others. He loved you so people would know who he is—a God of love.

Remember that all the members of your team have a common goal: to bring others to know Christ. God's desire is that all people will be saved. You can be a part of this work of God simply by loving your team members as you serve together.

Read Colossians 3:12-14. God gives us some ways to love as his chosen people, God's team. Which of the following do you need to work on most: compassion, kindness, humility, gentleness, patience, or forgiveness? How can you begin to love people more, especially those closest to you? How could loving the team members on your mission trip affect other people's lives?

Here are a few ways that you can show love to your team today:

- Look for the best in people, and tell them what you see!

- Treat them with grace.

- Admit when you are wrong.

• Pray for your teammates individually.

Think of some other ways that you can love your teammates, and put those into action today!

Thank God for the mission trip team you are a part of and what you can learn from each member of that team. Commit to putting aside your selfishness and pride. Make every effort to clothe yourself with compassion, kindness, humility, gentleness, and patience. Ask God to help you bear with any team member who threatens your patience. And ask God to reveal his love to other people through the love you and your teammates show for each other.

My Experience

My Experience

THE FOUR "EVERS"

by Keith Golubski

During this mission trip you have been challenged to serve: *whatever* God wanted, *whomever* he prepared for you to reach, *whenever* he asked, and *wherever* he sent you. These four "evers" are played out in our lives every day; we just don't always look for them. Here's how they played out in the life of Joseph.

WHATEVER

As you look at the life of Joseph, you can see that he did whatever he needed to do to serve God. One of the gifts he had was interpreting dreams. Although early on when he interpreted his dreams for his brothers, he was a little smug about it, and his brothers ended up throwing him into a pit and selling him into slavery! (Genesis 37). But later he got it right and used the gift for good.

After he was sold into slavery in Egypt, Joseph managed all the affairs of Potiphar's house. (Potiphar was one of Pharaoh's officials.) Joseph did this so well that Potiphar didn't even have to check up on him.

"When his master saw that the LORD was with him and that the LORD gave him success in everything he did, Joseph found favor in his eyes and became his attendant. Potiphar put him in charge of his household, and he entrusted to his care everything he owned. . . . with Joseph in charge, he did not concern himself with anything except the food he ate" (Genesis 39:3, 4, 6).

When Joseph was thrown into prison by his master for a crime he didn't commit

(vv. 6-20), he was so faithful to God that
the warden put him in charge of everyone
and everything in the prison (vv. 20-23).
Then Joseph's job changed again once he
interpreted Pharaoh's dreams (Genesis 41:1-38).
He was placed in a position second only to
Pharaoh (Genesis 41:39, 40).

During all of these situations, Joseph did
whatever he could to serve and work hard.
When he was sold into slavery, he did such
a good job as a slave that he was promoted
to the highest position in his master's house.
When he was in prison, he served to the
best of his ability and became responsible
for everything that took place in the prison.
When he was released from prison, he served
so well that he won Pharaoh's favor.

Joseph did not allow any of his trials
to overcome his desire to serve the Lord.
Joseph served in whatever capacity he was

placed. God blessed Joseph because of his faithfulness.

When you think about service, do not assume that it is something that doesn't matter. Yet on the other hand, do not see it as something huge and spectacular either. See it simply as your opportunity to honor the Lord.

What is the first thing you see when you look at a task you're given on your mission trip? Is it tempting to place projects on a category of important or not important? How can you look for ways to serve in whatever capacity you're able rather than wait for projects to be brought to you?

WHOMEVER

Imagine that you have been betrayed by your brothers, sold into slavery, and shipped to another land, language, and culture. You are now the property of someone else. You must obey orders—some of which you probably will not even understand! While all this is happening, your body is trying to adjust to the climate of a new land.

Through all his transitions, Joseph found a way to serve whomever was around him. Joseph did such a good job serving, as if serving for the Lord, that it was recognized. Potiphar, the prison warden, and Pharaoh saw that there was a true God and that Joseph obeyed God.

When you serve others, not just because you feel sorry for them or because you are obligated to or because you work for them, they see pure intentions. When we learn to see people with God's eyes, we see past the situations and see the souls God has created. We see people that God sent his Son to die for. We see people that have value and worth, people worthy to be served no matter what their outsides look like. We see what God sees.

When you look at other people, what is your first assumption? How can you adopt a "whomever" mentality on this mission trip?

WHENEVER

When we serve, most of the time we get to choose the time that's best for us. When you signed up for your trip, you probably checked to see if you had anything else to do during that time. When you see someone who needs help, do you see what you have going on first?

Joseph did not concern himself with his own agenda, most of all because he was a slave, or servant. He did not allow time for sulking to interfere with serving. Whenever he was put into a situation, he started doing what he did best—following God faithfully.

While Joseph was doing his usual duties in the prison one morning, he came across the cupbearer and the baker, who were dejected (Genesis 40). Right then and there, Joseph stopped what he was doing and attended to them. He did not say, "I've got work to do. You figure it out." Joseph interpreted their dreams and served them.

Two years later, the same situation arose when Pharaoh had a dream that no one could interpret. Finally the cupbearer mentioned Joseph. "So Pharaoh sent for Joseph, and he was quickly brought from the dungeon. When he had shaved and changed his clothes, he came before Pharaoh" (Genesis 41:14).

Joseph didn't have much choice in being brought before Pharaoh, but instead of taking his time with the interpretations or bargaining for his own freedom before interpreting the dreams, he did what he was asked to do. Then Pharaoh honored him:

"Pharaoh said to Joseph, 'Since God has made all this known to you, there is no one so discerning and wise as you. You shall be in charge of my palace, and all my people are to submit to your orders. Only with respect to the throne will I be greater than you'" (Genesis 41:39, 40).

When we try to serve only when it's convenient for us, we miss out on so many other opportunities. Not only do we miss out on a chance to serve, but people miss out on getting their needs met. You see, these opportunities aren't there just for you. God has set them up because someone has a need to be met by part of the body of Christ. If you pass that up, you leave someone out to dry, whether it's a physical need or a need to see Christ's love lived out.

Have you ever thought about how important timing is when it comes to serving people? Have you ever passed up an opportunity to serve because you had something else going on? How can you keep a "whenever" way of thinking during the rest of your trip?

WHEREVER

Joseph also served wherever he was. Joseph was taken far from anything he knew. He was a stranger in a foreign place. In everything Joseph did, God was with him. He became the most trusted person in Potiphar's house.

Then one person's lie put Joseph in prison, and later the lack of integrity in two other people kept him there. Even when you serve people and do what is right in the eyes of God, sometimes you will face persecution. People will try to bring you down, but in Joseph's case, he rose above it all and served the warden of the jail. This again brought attention, not just to Joseph but to God. The warden saw that God was with him.

Two years later, Pharaoh was troubled by some dreams. Finally they called on Joseph to interpret them; and because God was with him, he did. Not only did Joseph interpret the dreams, he was placed in a high position to oversee the storing up of food before the famine.

As you look at the times in Joseph's life that everyone considers the worst, those times were when he saw God's best. Wherever he was, Joseph found a way to follow God. He found God in a cistern. He found God in Egypt. He found God in prison. He found God as Pharaoh's most trusted official. In each of the places where he had never planned on being, he served God—and did it so well that people noticed.

Have you ever been somewhere that you never expected to be? How did you react? Can look back now and see that God was there with you? What can you do to make sure that you are serving wherever you are placed on this mission trip?

ALL YOUR "EVERS"

As you strive to serve God whatever, whomever, whenever, and wherever on your trip, thank God for allowing you to be used in his service. And remember that others are seeing God through your actions.

My Experience

BE A BRANCH

by Kevin Greer

If you knew you had only hours to live, how would you spend that time? With whom would you want to spend that time? What's some of the best advice about life that you've ever been given?

JESUS' ADVICE

In John 15:1-10, Jesus uses some of his final words to give advice to the people nearest and dearest to him. Scholars believe these words were spoken on the night of the last supper. The night of betrayal.

Jesus likely spoke these words while walking from the upper room to the Garden of Gethsemane. Perhaps he saw a vine hanging over a fence or draped along the wall. Perhaps as he lifted up a section of the plant, he spoke the words from John 15 to explain the chain of command in the universe: God is the gardener; Jesus is the vine; we are the branches that produce the grapes.

Vines grew abundantly in Palestine. Carefully pruned, they produced sweet grapes. But left untended, they crept everywhere and into everything. The gardener trimmed the vines. Why? So they could bear more fruit. God "trims" us. Why? For the same reason.

A good gardener will do what it takes to help a vine bear fruit. What fruit does God want? "Love, joy, peace, patience, kindness, goodness, faithfulness, gentleness and self-control" (Galatians 5:22, 23). These are the fruits of the Spirit—meaning, they are the characteristics that should be evident in our lives if we are allowing God's Holy Spirit to take control. And this is what God longs to see in us. Like a careful gardener, he will clip and cut away anything that interferes.

PRUNING OUR LIVES

Clipping, cutting, trimming . . . these aren't terms that bring about pleasant thoughts when applied to my life. I don't think I like the idea of pain and sacrifice. But I want things to be better, don't I? Then I must realize that improvement often involves sacrifice, time, effort, and pain.

God lifts up a branch of his vine and says, "You can be fruitful, but I'm going to have to clip some diseased branches." The process is painful. We can look on the ground below us to see the diseased branches he has clipped. In hindsight, we can look back and see how God used circumstances, people, and so on to cut away arrogance, selfish ambitions, bad relationships, dangerous opportunities, and revenge.

So the gardener (that's God), cuts away at the branches (that's you and me). Why does he do that? Look again at John 15:2. He does it so the branches will bear fruit. *Fruit* is one of those funny Bible terms that can be easily explained. God wants us to bear fruit, which means he wants us to *do something*!

"REMAIN IN ME"

But a branch can't make grapes on its own. You can't force fruit. You can't willpower your way into God's kingdom. That's why nowhere in this chapter does Jesus command you to go out and make some fruit. That's right. Nowhere! God cuts the branches *so* they can be ready to hold the fruit God makes, but nowhere does Jesus command us to make fruit. Look for yourself.

So what *does* he command us to do?

1. "Remain in me" (v. 4).

2. "Remain in the vine" (v. 4).

3. "Remain in me, and I in them" (v. 5, *NLT*).

4. "Remain in me" (v. 6).

5. "Remain in me" (v. 7).

6. "Remain in my love" (v. 9).

7. "Remain in my love" (v. 10).

Our task is pretty clear: stay close to the vine. As long as we do, we'll be fruitful. Life comes through the vine. Apart from the vine, the branch can do nothing. Jesus says it himself in verse 5.

SO WHAT DO I DO?

So what does that mean for you on your mission trip? Well, it means that you can serve all you want and do a lot of good deeds, but unless you are connected to Jesus and following his direction and serving for God's glory, you will not produce the fruit God intends.

But this Scripture also means you are free from carrying the big load. In other words, you don't have to do it all yourself! You don't have to save the world. Jesus took care of that. You don't have to convict people of their wrong ways. The Holy Spirit takes care of that. You don't have to know all the answers and fix all of life's problems. God is taking care of that. All you have to do is be a branch that stays tight with the vine, and God's fruit will be produced through you. Or to translate, all you need to do is live as a follower of Jesus and spend time with him in order to grow, and God will produce faithful actions and words in your life as a result.

What is keeping you from being faithful to God? In other words, what are some branches that need to be cut from your life? Ask God to come and cut those branches away.

Thank God for producing the fruit and allowing you to bear it on his behalf. Commit to remaining in Jesus, the vine, during your mission trip—and once you return home too.

My Experience

TRUST
AND OBEY

by Lindsey Miller

We had finally landed in Sao Paulo,
Brazil—the flight there had been a
nightmare. What was supposed to be a
nonstop, seven-and-a-half-hour flight turned
into a sixteen-hour flight with three stops.

The overhead compartments had to
be shut with duct tape, the lights and air
vents were not working (to conserve power,
we learned later), and the flight crew was
incredibly rude. You know the seatbelt
presentation you get on a flight before
takeoff? We never got it—all three departure
times! One of our stops was supposed to be
in Manaus, a city in northern Brazil. As we

approached, the pilot reported that we were going to have to divert to another airport close by, as another pilot had just crashed on the runway because he didn't put down the wheels of the plane in order to land. This posed the question: When we land, will our pilot remember to put down *our* plane's wheels?

We missed our connecting flight by hours, and once we made it through a stress-filled customs experience, we headed to the main terminal to see what the airline would do for us. The whole situation was, after all, their fault. We had no idea what we were about to encounter. Hundreds of other people were in the same situation as our group.

Tempers were flaring, people were stressed, and the airlines were all but helpful. We came to discover they had declared bankruptcy during our flight. Not what you want to hear when you're in a foreign airport, surrounded by angry individuals!

As the other team leader and I tried to figure out how to get our group to our final mission trip destination, we began to wonder whether we would spend the next couple of weeks in the Sao Paulo airport.

WITH ALL YOUR HEART

Trust—it can be a very hard thing for us to do at times. It requires us to acknowledge that we don't know everything, that we can't handle things on our own, and that we don't have everything figured out. It requires us to put our faith in someone or something else. Our independent, self-sufficient sides don't like this idea.

"Trust in the LORD with all your heart and lean not on your own understanding;

in all your ways acknowledge him, and he will make your paths straight" (Proverbs 3:5, 6). These are verses that many of us may have memorized and could say in our sleep. But does this mean we really understand this important truth? If we did, then wouldn't our lives be radically different from the lives of people around us? What does it look like to actually trust in the Lord with all your heart?

DESTINATION UNKNOWN

The life of Abraham paints a great picture of trust for us. Read Genesis 12:1-8 and Hebrews 11:8-10. Abraham trusted God and left. He left his home, his people, his comforts—his life really, "even though he did not know where he was going" (Hebrews 11:8).

Can you imagine this? You left your home to serve on this mission trip. However, you knew where you were going! And you probably had been preparing to leave for months. Not the case with Abraham. He trusted God and left, even though he didn't know whether to pack mosquito repellant or snowshoes. Another little fact I find interesting: Genesis 12:4 says that Abraham was seventy-five when he left his home. He was past retirement age!

What things did you leave to come on this trip? What are some things you still need to leave behind to fully trust in what God is calling you to do?

BELIEVING WITHOUT SEEING

Let's keep reading: Genesis 15:1-6; Genesis 21:2, 3; and Hebrews 11:11, 12. Abraham trusted God and believed. God told Abraham that he was going to be the father of many nations, and his descendants became as numerous as the stars in the sky and the sand on the seashore.

There sat Abraham, age 100, still with no children. But God continued to remind Abraham of his promise, and Abraham believed! He believed that God was all-powerful and that his word was true. Even when circumstances weren't looking his way, Abraham believed in who God was. And did you catch what Genesis 15:6 says about Abraham's belief? It was credited to him "as righteousness."

Take a few moments to think about who God is. What do you need to believe as you trust in who God is? What is holding you back?

SACRIFICE REQUIRED

Finally, Abraham trusted God even when it required sacrifice. Read Genesis 22:1-18 and Hebrews 11:17-19. What a crazy story. I can't help but wonder if Abraham was thinking, *Are you kidding right now, God? You promised I would be the father of many nations. You have given me a son, and now you want me to sacrifice him? What in the world is going on here?*

But Abraham trusted. He was willing to sacrifice everything because he believed in God. Look again at what Abraham said to Isaac in Genesis 22:8 when Isaac asked him about the lamb needed for the offering: "God himself will provide." Even when Abraham couldn't see how God would provide, he still obeyed.

What things do you need to sacrifice? What is holding you back from being fully obedient to the almighty God?

GOD WAS WATCHING OVER US

We did make it out of the Sao Paulo airport and to our final destination that night of our mission trip. But God provided in ways we couldn't have predicted.

There were at least a hundred people on the waiting list to get on the final flight of the night with another airline. The other leader and I were standing in the rebooking line, waiting to see what the really nice airline agent could do for us, while the team members prayed in a circle in the crowded terminal.

The agent was feverishly typing away on her little screen, speaking to other airline workers on her walkie-talkie to see what they knew. She spoke to us in a combination of Portuguese, English, and Spanish phrases and updated us every three seconds on what she could offer. Maybe three seats tonight, four seats on another flight in the morning, and four seats on the evening flight tomorrow?

This wasn't going to work because it still left us two seats short. Plus we couldn't justify leaving already nervous students alone in a foreign airport.

All of a sudden, she stopped. Her face turned a little pale, and she looked at us and said, "Thirteen seats. They just opened up. I can't even explain . . . they weren't here a few minutes ago . . . how did this hap—" We didn't even let her finish her sentence. "We'll take them!" we shouted. After thanking her at least a thousand times and telling her she was one of our favorite people, we headed to our gate and flew out of the crazy ordeal.

The next morning, we were sipping our coffee with the hosting missionary, discussing the whole mess. (We still weren't quite laughing about it at this point.) What we hadn't seen that night while we were stuck in the airport was the Brazilian team we were to join up with. When they heard about our team stuck in the Sao Paulo airport, they had immediately started praying for us. As we talked, we figured out that they were praying, along with our students, during the time that the seats "magically" opened up for us. Cool, huh?

WAYS YOU DON'T UNDERSTAND

God was at work during our traveling troubles in ways we couldn't even see, imagine, or explain. God is working in ways you don't understand right now on your mission trip and in your life. God is so much bigger than your little world. He is calling you to step outside yourself and trust in his power and goodness. Will you?

Will you, like Abraham, leave your comforts, believe in who God is, and sacrifice what is most important to you? Will you trust?

Take a few moments to pray through Proverbs 3:5, 6: "God, today I trust in you with ALL of my heart, and I will lean not on my own understanding. In all that I do, I will acknowledge you as you make my paths straight. I don't know what that looks like, and it may not make sense to my brain. But, God, I want to trust. Help me today as I trust and obey you with all that I am."

My Experience

QUIET SERVICE

by Katie Runner

When was the last time you did something good so that others would take notice? I recently had a close friend e-mail me to say, "I accepted Christ! God works in the most unusual and best ways, and I now believe in him!" I was ecstatic.

I immediately e-mailed and called my friends to let them know that my dear friend we had been praying for had become a Christian. As I was telling more people, I found my thoughts turning more and more to me. *Look what I have done. My time with her and constant prayers for her finally accomplished something.* I wanted my friends to know how much I had done in this new Christian's life.

When it hit me how I was acting, I questioned my motives. Why did I want to tell my friends about this girl's decision to obey Christ? Obviously, I wanted them to rejoice with me. But there was a part of me that wanted them to see the impact that all of my love and prayers had made. Realizing what I was doing, I stopped my selfish train of thought.

Who am I to claim anything anyway? It is not as though her salvation had anything to do with me. God alone had been at work in her heart. I needed to set my selfish thoughts aside and rejoice in the work of God.

SEEKING RECOGNITION

How many times do you do something so that others will nod their heads and say, "Yes, she really loves people" or "Wow, he sure is a good person"? There is a deep desire in all of us to be noticed. We crave approval and recognition from people.

It's OK to receive some recognition at times, but other times no one is going to notice that you spent all that time serving, praying, giving, or fasting. Sometimes not being noticed is the way it should be or will be. In fact, this is the way that Jesus desires. Read Matthew 6:1-18.

Take some time to examine your life right now: How do you pray? How are you with your money? Do you fast? Did you know that there are different kinds of fasts other than fasting from food (for example, fasting from music, TV, etc.)?

How does Jesus say we should do all of these things? When you pray, give, and fast, why do you do it?

SERVING IN THE SHADOWS

Most people recognize the name of Oswald Chambers, a man who has inspired millions through the years by his most famous book, *My Utmost for His Highest*. Most people do not recognize the name of Biddy Chambers, Oswald's wife. As you discover more about Oswald's life, you come to find that the pages of devotionals in this book would not be in print if his wife Biddy had not worked hard for years.

Every time Oswald preached or led devotions, Biddy would faithfully take precise notes. It was these notes that were later used to publish the devotional that has challenged and encouraged many people. No one ever gave Oswald's wife recognition for all of her service for God, yet her work has changed millions of lives.

I would say that the best work you do is done where no eye can see. Then you have the joy of knowing that you are serving God only.

Ask yourself: What motivates me today to serve on this mission trip? How am I going to change my perspective and love people—not to be recognized but simply because God has poured his love into me?

If you will, pray this prayer or something similar as you strive to serve humbly without recognition:

"Father, as I serve you today, help me to love people because that is what you want. Help me not to seek the notice of other people in the things I do. I want to be willing to do those tasks that seem small and unimportant, the ones no one else wants to do. God, I want to serve today on this mission trip, not in my name but in your name. Amen."

My Experience

BEFORE AND AFTER

by Ben Hedger

When your mission trip started, there were probably a hundred projects to be completed. Buildings will have cracking paint, overgrown brush, dingy walls, sagging porches, and anxious occupants. Children's VBS programs will need to be set up with the proper location, advertisement, and supplies.

Each group arrives at its mission destination able to see what needs to take place. Team members scrape old paint off walls, cut down unwanted brush, apply fresh paint, and reinforce weak boards. They visit with people, pray with strangers, and teach children.

The BEFORE picture is neither very inviting nor something to be desired. However, the completed task brings smiles and joy to those who are blessed by your efforts.

CHANGED LIVES

As you serve others, think about the BEFORE and AFTER picture. People that you help may not have hope as they live each day. Some are full of sadness because they are unable to take care of their homes or they have other physical needs. Some ministries are worn thin, the leaders questioning whether they have the means to keep going. But when you lend a hand, people receive hope and joy. A ministry is rejuvenated and ready to keep rolling because of your willingness to help.

The BEFORE picture reminds you of when you were without hope and the love of God. The AFTER picture reveals that God's love is powerful. Remember how your life changed when God entered the scene. This is the same impact that you will have on those you serve today. How great it is to partner with God as he creates the AFTER picture because of servant-minded people like you.

Consider a drastic BEFORE and AFTER picture from Scripture by looking at Saul, later called Paul. He went from persecuting those who believed in Jesus to preaching to others about Jesus! (Acts 8:1-3; 9:1-31). His life was totally changed once he met Christ.

What did your mission trip project look like BEFORE you started? What has your group been doing in order to assist the physical and spiritual needs of people around you?

HUMBLE SERVICE

A mission trip to India introduced me to people who know what it means to serve. I'm talking five-star service, the royal treatment. It can be labeled service with a capital *S*. Our hosts prepared and served our meals each day, all the while making sure that our needs were met. The level of servanthood they displayed humbled our team.

The service of our hosts challenged us to evaluate our own actions. Were we putting ourselves so fully into our service?

Look at the times when you have experienced something similar. Maybe you have been to a restaurant and the service was excellent. Every time you took a drink, your glass was full, and all the extras were taken care of without a request by you. Perhaps you were on the giving end of such treatment. Maybe you took it upon yourself to go the extra mile and bring a level of joy and happiness to some people that they might not have experienced BEFORE.

LASTING RESULTS

When we take on this type of servant attitude, a couple of things happen. First, the relationship between people develops stronger and quicker. The friendships we made with the people from India who served our meals was a blessing. BEFORE we interacted with them on a nightly basis, we were strangers. AFTER, we were friends. You can be a blessing as you build a strong friendship with those you serve.

The second blessing of humble servitude is that it allows more tasks to be accomplished for God. Our team had the possibility of speaking with more Indian students because of the friendship we built.

We met people who hadn't known Jesus BEFORE we arrived. AFTER we got to know them, we were able to tell them about God's grace. If we had not built such a strong friendship through their service to us, it may have become more difficult to share God's love with them.

In Acts 9:36-42 we read of a woman whose incredible servant attitude developed tight bonds with others. Tabitha touched many lives, and the sadness of her friends when she died spoke volumes about her service and generosity. Many rejoiced and followed Jesus when they heard Tabitha had been raised from the dead.

What friendships have you made on this mission trip because of your service? Have you been served by anyone else on this trip? How did that bond you together?

SERVANT PRAYERS

Spend some time thinking about the changes you've seen during your mission trip—the spiritual BEFORE and AFTER that has happened so far. Pray that God will give you the chance to be a part of life change that will bring about a beautiful AFTER picture.

Also consider the bonds of friendship that you've formed and strengthened by serving others. Pray that your service will continue to build friendships with those you help.

My Experience

TRUE LOVE

by Andrea Butterbaugh

Do you know what true love is? Did you know that people are watching how you treat fellow believers? Your actions of love toward fellow believers are part of your testimony to the world. And what about loving those who aren't yet in God's family? Have you considered that your choice to love them will have a positive influence on them, not to mention *you* as well?

"IF"

Read the following passages: John 13:34, 35; John 14:15, 23, 24; John 15:9-17. Love is a choice. If you look closely at these Scriptures, you will see that Jesus made use of the word *if* frequently. Wait. Jesus was sharing one of his last messages with his disciples, and he left them with *if*? Yes, Jesus told them (and tells us!) what would happen *if* they love him, *if* they obey his commands, and *if* they remain in him.

Our side of the love equation is a choice, but Jesus' side is a promise. If we love him, we will obey his commands (John 14:15). If we obey his commands, we will remain in his love (15:10). If we do what he commands, we will be his friends (15:14). He ended the discussion with a simple and direct statement: "This is my command: Love each other" (15:17).

Jesus gave a clear picture of what this love means when he said, "Greater love has no one than this, that he lay down his life for his friends" (John 15:13). This is the kind of love we are to share. It is a love of total devotion. It is willful, it is unconditional, and it is a choice. We are called to share it with one another and with the world.

DEMONSTRATION FROM THE TEACHER

But before Jesus told his disciples these things, he had already demonstrated the extent of his love by washing their feet (John 13). He lived out sincere, devoted, total love as an example to them. Then he told them to go out and live that same way.

Jesus' loving demonstration was a parallel to the humility he was soon to display on the cross—as he did lay down his life for his friends.

The challenge to us is discovering how we carry this out in day-to-day life. How do we choose to love over and over again, each day? How will you show love to your fellow team members, your host missionaries, or a stranger on the road?

And how do we find the intensity of love that God calls us to? It's tough, but it's expected—and it's necessary if we are going to allow the Lord to shine through us in this dark world.

AUNT T. T.

One year I was in Indianapolis for the National Missionary Convention. I had been encouraged to spend more time getting to know the down-and-out of our society. As I walked through the streets of downtown Indianapolis, I was feeling a gentle prodding of the Spirit to sit with a homeless person, maybe even take that person to dinner.

I saw a woman sitting on a milk crate, shaking her cup and begging for change. Not that I have an extreme amount of exposure to homeless beggars, but this was the first time I had ever seen an older female sitting on a street corner and shaking her cup.

She could be safe, I thought, but there was a homeless man standing by her, talking to her. As I moved toward her, I debated whether or not this was something I should do. And as the moment came, I passed her by.

Within seconds after I passed her, the man with her left also, and he and I wound up standing at the same intersection, waiting for the light to change. I have a rule I follow when I meet homeless people on the street. I always make eye contact and smile, and often I will speak. So I made eye contact and smiled at this man. He responded.

We ended up walking back toward the woman on the milk crate, and he introduced me to "Aunt T. T." (That wasn't her real name but her street name. I learned that her real name was Joyce.) The man moved on, but I sat on the street corner and talked with Aunt T. T. for a long time. She taught me about life on the streets. We laughed together a lot and shared dinner together on the street corner before I left.

Aunt T. T. was the first one to mention God that night. When it came time for me to leave, Aunt T. T. laid her hand on my shoulder and looked me in the eyes—she was a little teary-eyed—and said, "I want to ask God to bless you. I know he is going to bless you, and he will be with you wherever you go. He will always be right there with you, taking care of you."

Initially, I had felt I needed to sit with a homeless person so I could minister to her and show her Jesus. But I think when all was said and done, she had ministered to me.

CHOOSE LOVE

Today, don't neglect the choice to love your brothers and sisters in Christ or to love people you've just met. Is it difficult for you to love someone on your team, someone with whom you should share the love demonstrated by Christ when he laid down his life for you? Tell God where your weaknesses lie, and pray for him to help you through your issues and to help you show love to that person today.

Have you had the opportunity to show love to a stranger on this trip through some small act of selfless service? Did you act on the opportunity God gave you, or did you pass by? Ask God's forgiveness for the times you neglected to love, and ask him to give you the courage to take every new chance he puts before you.

Thank God for the ability to love. And as you go through this day, and the rest of your journey in Christ, remember that you can choose love—true love—every day.

My Experience

HURRY, HURRY, HURRY

by Pat Fancher

My typical day begins with noise: alarm clock ringing, dogs barking outside, sirens blaring, music playing on the radio, and sounds of people talking. Added to this mix is an endless monologue swirling through my head—things I need to accomplish today along with snippets of conversations from yesterday. My day is a sea of endless noise and motion, a sense of "hurry up, time's a-wastin'."

Noise affects human behavior. During experiments in Los Angeles, researchers found that children who lived in neighborhoods near the airport could not—when jets were landing and taking off—complete certain tasks as easily as children who lived in quiet neighborhoods.

In another experiment carried out by psychologists, a student leaving a library intentionally dropped an armload of books. In 50 percent of the cases, a passerby stopped to help the student pick up the books. Then the experimenters brought out a lawn mower without a muffler and started it near where a student again deliberately dropped the books. This time, only about 10 percent of the people who passed stopped to help. It was clear that behavior changed because of the earsplitting sound of the nearby lawn mower.

A HURRIED LIFESTYLE

It's not just noise that disrupts our peace. Unfortunately, our society promotes a hurried lifestyle: fast food, one-hour photos, express lunches, electronic refunds, quick cash, and more. In such a fast-paced culture, you have to be intentional about slowing down.

I suffer from "hurry sickness." Frequently I am in a rush—even when I don't know where I am going. Recently our family was planning to go to a newly released movie, and we decided to purchase our tickets in advance. My husband pulled up to the curb by the movie theater, and I jetted over to the ticket window. Then with our tickets tightly grasped in my hand, I ran blindly to our red SUV. Or I should say, what I *thought* was our SUV.

I opened the door and jumped onto the passenger seat. When I glanced over at the driver, it was not my husband but an amused stranger sitting behind the wheel. With a big smile on his face, the driver said, "Well, hello there!" After mumbling an embarrassed apology, I managed to open the door and flee to our vehicle, which was parked directly behind. My family laughed shamelessly at my mistake!

I need to slow down and seek quiet moments to refresh both my heart and spirit.

BREAKING THE HURRY CYCLE

Through his prophets, God admonished his people to return to him—to repent, rest, be quiet, and trust in him. Yet they didn't and brought harm on themselves. "In repentance and rest is your salvation, in quietness and trust is your strength, but you would have none of it" (Isaiah 30:15).

Jesus was also aware of the dangers of a hurried life. He repeatedly withdrew from crowds and taught his disciples to do the same. To practice solitude. Jesus told them, "Let's go off by ourselves to a quiet place and rest awhile" (Mark 6:31, *NLT*).

Jesus often had much to do, but he never did it in a way that severed the life-giving connection between him and his Father. And his time alone never interfered with his ability to give love when love was called for. He observed a regular practice of withdrawing from activity for the sake of solitude and prayer.

ASSESS YOUR HURRIEDNESS

Are you constantly on the fast track and find it difficult to slow down long enough to have intimate moments each day with God? Has that hurried attitude spilled over onto this mission trip? Have you had an opportunity to share your faith but because of your own busyness, you did not take the time? In what ways can you change your life, beginning today, to seek solitude with God?

Seek a quiet spot where you can be uninterrupted and without distractions.

Spend some time just being still and quieting your mind. Offer a prayer of thanksgiving to God for his love. Ask him to cover you with his peace and grace. Ask him to give you a deeper love and compassion for those who do not know him.

My Experience

FINDING CONTENTMENT

by Ben Hedger

Many people find it hard to be content with their lives. They seek fulfillment in areas that will never satisfy. Searching through books, surfing the Internet, and watching television shows do not offer the right answers. Desiring to have the lifestyle of another is not healthy. On the other hand, some people, to feel content, just need a roof over their heads and to be surrounded by the people they love. This situation does help a person feel protected and comforted. However, do even these basic things truly bring contentment?

A SECRET

In Philippians 4:12, 13, Paul said, "I have learned the secret of being content in any and every situation, whether well fed or hungry, whether living in plenty or in want. I can do everything through him who gives me strength."

What is the secret to contentment? Being content can be found in the relationships that you form. Through associations with others you find wisdom, love, and encouragement. But as Paul discovered, lasting contentment can only be found in the most important relationship, your relationship with Christ. It did not matter whether Paul had food or clothing, as long as he had a connection with Christ. Because of his relationship with Christ, Paul did not worry about his next meal or a warm place to sleep. We can experience that same contentment with Jesus.

Although Paul discovered what brings contentment, this is not true for many people. Often contentment is associated with financial stability. For those people, as long as the money is there to purchase items they need or want, everything is fine. Well, for a while maybe. A focus on wealth at any level can lead people to be discontent. Remember that possessions collected here on earth will not go with us when we leave (1 Timothy 6:6-10). The "secret of being content" isn't really a secret—it only remains a secret when Christ is absent from people's lives.

EXAMINE YOUR PERSPECTIVE

You will encounter situations in life that cause you to examine your perspective on contentment. Certainly being part of your mission trip has opened your eyes. You have probably seen people with little food and very poor shelter. Do you think those families have the same view of contentment that Paul did? They can if you tell them. You may see children running to your side with smiles that melt your heart. Do they know the joy that Paul had in all situations? If not, share that secret of contentment!

As you serve on your mission trip, remember that even if you are caring for people's physical needs, the only way to guide them to true contentment is by providing for their spiritual needs too. Teach them about Jesus, and they will be able to persevere in the trials of life.

Do you ever find your contentment in people or possessions? How can you change your perspective? What events on this mission trip have helped you to realize what contentment is all about? How can you keep that attitude of contentment with you once you go home from this trip?

Spend some time in prayer. Talk to God about your past and current attitudes in the area of contentment. Confess the times when you've been tempted to want more than you need. Ask God to keep reminding you that he is the only way to true contentment. Ask him to teach that truth to the people you have met on this mission trip.

My Experience

BROKEN HEARTS

by Amy Sackett

Hearts are my thing—literally. As a nurse, for twelve hours a day, three days a week, I try to mend broken hearts. But the hardest part of my job is helping people to embrace the fact that their hearts are hurting.

We have a tendency to run from pain. We do not like to be uncomfortable, we do not like to be inconvenienced, and we certainly do not like to ask for help. Unfortunately for my patients, heart attacks are not something that you can run from too easily. It is the kind of pain that grabs your attention and will not let go until you have addressed it.

I have seen other types of broken hearts as well. Over the years, having been a student and a leader for mission trips, I have seen team members grab at their chests, trying to shake off what they have seen or what they are experiencing. It is uncomfortable to see other people in pain and poverty. It is inconvenient to sleep on the floor and resonate with those around you. And it is hard to ask for help when you are struggling with the new culture you are facing.

But that discomfort has a purpose. When a person is having physical pain, it is a warning that something is wrong. When you are having emotional or spiritual pain, it is a warning that there is something to which you need to pay attention.

Maybe it is a reaction to your surroundings. It may hurt you to look into the faces of the three billion people who live on less than two dollars a day. Or it may bother you that you are conserving water right now, but that on average you use one hundred seventy gallons every day at home. It may sting to think that Americans spend billions of dollars annually on ice cream—think of all the hungry children that amount of money could feed.

You may never have faced this kind of poverty before. You may never have faced this kind of hunger before or lack of education or . . . take your pick of a number of things that may be swimming around in your head. Or maybe you are being confronted with your own heart, with your own pride. It hurts to look inside and see the filth that we bring along with us. We bring our arrogance, our wealth, our security. It is hard when our comfortable culture clashes with someone else's.

The question is, what will you do with that pain? What will you do when your heart hurts, when it is breaking? Will you try to shove the pain aside and pretend that everything is OK? Will you try to put patches and temporary fixes on the hurt? Or will you allow God to break your heart all the way? Because with change comes brokenness before rebuilding.

When my husband and I moved into our house a few years ago, we discovered a large leak coming from our upstairs bathroom. My husband needed to rip out the entire bathroom, down to the studs in the walls. Was that remodeling? Not exactly. That was demolition.

Has some demolition taken place in your heart during this mission trip? Are there things that you do not quite understand or that you just cannot process? What will your next step be? Will you embrace the things that God is showing you and allow him to remodel your heart? If you allow him full access, you will become a different person. Your actions will be different. You will head home from this trip with a different perspective and goal. You will begin to see the things that break God's heart, and you will not run from taking action.

To close out your mission trip, please read Psalm 51 and make it your prayer to God. Especially focus on verses 10-17. Tell God what is breaking your heart, and ask him to rebuild it by making it more like his. Seek his wisdom and strength so that you can continue to be a part of reaching the world for Jesus as you head back home.

My Experience

_____

_____

_____

_____

_____

_____

_____

_____

_____

_____

_____

_____

_____

_____

_____